Self-Pollination

by Jennifer Boothroyd

first step nonfiction

Lerner Publications · Minneapolis

Copyright © 2015 by Lerner Publishing Group, Inc.

The images in this book are used with the permission of: © Sodapix/Thinkstock, p. 4; © vencavolrab/iStock/Thinkstock, p. 5; © iStockphoto.com/bkkm, p. 6; © TongRo Images/Thinkstock, p. 7; © HandmadePictures/iStock/Thinkstock, p. 7 (inset); © iStockphoto.com/Risto0, p. 8; © DEA/C. DANI/I.JESKE/De Agostini/Getty Images, p. 9; © Greg Dimijian/Photo Researchers/Getty Images, p. 10; © iStockphoto.com/Mantonature, p. 11; © blickwinkel/Alamy, p. 12; © Ron Evans/Getty Images, p. 13; © Alan Majchrowicz/Photolibrary/Getty Images, p. 14; © Kevin Schafer/Alamy, p. 15; © S-e-v-e-r-e/iStock/Thinkstock, p. 16; © iStockphoto.com/hüseyin harmandaglı, p. 17; © iStockphoto.com/Nancy Nehring, p. 18; © Wayne Lynch/All Canada Photos/Alamy, p. 19; © WILDLIFE GmbH/Alamy, p. 20; © Anne Gilbert/Alamy, p. 21; © KPG_Payless/Shutterstock.comp. 22. Front cover: © Vladimir Melnik/Shutterstock.com.

Main body text set in ITC Avant Garde Gothic Std Medium 21/25.
Typeface provided by Adobe Systems.

Lerner Publications Company
A division of Lerner Publishing Group, Inc.
241 First Avenue North
Minneapolis, MN 55401 USA

For reading levels and more information, look up this title at www.lernerbooks.com.

Library of Congress Cataloging-in-Publication Data

Boothroyd, Jennifer, 1972–
    Self-pollination / by Jennifer Boothroyd.
      pages   cm. — (First step nonfiction - Pollination)
    Includes index.
    ISBN 978-1-4677-5740-9 (lib. bdg. : alk. paper)
    ISBN 978-1-4677-6227-4 (eBook)
    1. Self-pollination—Juvenile literature. I. Title. II. Series: First step nonfiction. Pollination.
QK926.B663 2015
571.8'642—dc23   2014019897

Manufactured in the United States of America
1 – CG – 12/31/14

Table of Contents

Pollination

Look at this bee. **Pollen** from a flower is sticking to its legs!

The pollen falling off this bee pollinates the new flower.

The bee flies to a different flower. This flower gets **pollinated**.

Most plants are pollinated with pollen from other plants.

Pollinated plants can grow seeds.

seeds

This kind of pollination is called **cross-pollination**.

English sundews make seeds using their own pollen.

Self-pollinating plants use their own pollen to grow seeds.

How Self-Pollination Works

Some self-pollinating plants live in places with extreme weather.

Few bees or other insects
can live in these spots.

Yellow rattle plants grow
where it is cold and dry.

Luckily, many self-pollinating plants do not need help from insects.

11

Pollen does not have to move far on these small bur clover flowers.

Self-pollinating plants often have smaller flowers.

The smaller size makes it easier for the plant to self-pollinate.

The pollen made by the plant rubs off inside the

flower.

Self-Pollinating Plants

Many kinds of plants self-pollinate.

Dandelions self-pollinate.

Tomato plants self-pollinate.

Soybeans self-pollinate.

Arctic poppies grow in Alaska.

Arctic poppies self-pollinate.

Lettuce pollinates
before the flowers open.

Lettuce self-pollinates.

Concord grapes self-pollinate.

Pollination is an important part of the life of a plant.

Glossary

cross-pollination – the movement of pollen from one flower to another flower

pollen – a powder made inside flowers

pollinated – marked or smudged with pollen

self-pollinating – plants that can use their own pollen to grow seeds

Index